HOW TO HEAL

A BROKEN HEART

Let Go Of Pain and Learn to Love Again

by
Carolyn Hughes

Table of Contents

Introduction

Everyone needs love in their life. And they need to be loved. Why? Because it's through love that you find your identity and worth. When you're struggling with the pain of a broken heart, it hits to the core of your mind, body, and soul.

This book is for anyone who has had their heart broken in the past or who is going through a heartbreak. Whether it's the loss of a loved one, a failed relationship, an abusive partner, or a family difficulty, the hurt is real.

As the founder and author of The Hurt Healer blog, there is one question that regularly appears in my messages and emails: "How do I heal my broken heart?" The answer is to find a way to let go of pain and learn to love again.

Healing is a process. It takes courage to heal, but over time it is possible to move from that place of pain to one of peace. When you act from a place of peace you make informed decisions and choices, you take responsibility for your life, you let go of the anger, and you learn to forgive. In doing so, you release yourself from the darkness of your past to move into the light of a new beginning. You move from feeling powerless to powerful.

How to Heal a Broken Heart can help you make the transition from broken-hearted to whole-hearted so that you are free to love again.

Chapter 1:
A Broken Heart

"We loved with a love that was more than love."
~ Edgar Allan Poe

Rejected by someone you love. Betrayed by a trusted friend. Lied to by the one person you thought you could rely on. Any of these can cause heartache. At some point in our lives, all of us are going to experience a broken heart. And while everyone's situation is different, and everyone's pain is unique, the one thing that holds true for all is that when your heart is broken, it hurts.

We all have relationships in our lives that come to a natural end. For whatever reason, our contact with that person runs its course. We move on without a sense of loss or pain. But there are other relationships that we continue to involve ourselves in, or that we cling to, in the hope that there will be a shift in commitment, interest, or behavior. And it's those interactions that we need to reflect on.

Then there are those relationships that we wish could last forever. Everyone has someone who plays an intrinsic part in their life. There is a bond that you never want broken. There is a uniqueness that you never want to share. Your relationship is special, it's precious, and it's all yours. Unthinkable, then, that one day you may have to live without your kindred soul; unimaginable that you may have to go through each day without the one that filled your heart. Yet it happens. It doesn't really matter how, the outcome is the same — you feel like you've lost a part of you and you'll never feel the same again.

The more time, energy, and emotion you've put in, the greater the pain. The more you believed in that person's integrity, honesty, or commitment, the more you are likely to feel that you'll never trust or love again. Giving your all can result in an extreme case of complete heartbreak. It doesn't matter if the love you've been mourning was lost years ago or more recently, the anguish can be just as intense.

"Love knows not its own depth until the hour of separation."
~ Khalil Gibran

As a young woman I went in search of my mother who had abandoned me as a child. Although she'd never physically been there for me as I grew up, she had been a daily presence in my mind. She was my flesh and blood, after all. My desire was simple — to have the opportunity to meet the woman I had cherished in my heart for as long as I could remember.

Nothing could have prepared me for the agony that ensued. I learned that my mother had a new family and that she'd explained my absence by telling everyone I'd been killed in a car crash. It didn't matter that I was alive and ready to pour out the special love I had treasured. To this woman I was dead.

Every fiber of my being wanted to meet her and touch her just once. But in reality there was no other option but to give up the search. You can't change the past. You can't open a door that is well and truly shut. And you can't make someone love you when they don't.

While I accepted the reality of my situation on many levels, I wouldn't allow myself to acknowledge the pain. But you can't change what you don't acknowledge. You may want to hibernate, hide, avoid the world, but that is exactly when you should hold your head up and face it. That's a harsh truth to face when you're vulnerable, yet it's also the truth that will set you on the path to emotional wholeness.

"We may get knocked down on the outside, but the key to living in victory is to learn how to get up on the inside." ~ Joel Osteen

The question for me, as it is for you, is: how do I heal my broken heart?

A broken heart results in a broken being. The world that previously existed shatters into a thousand pieces of hurt, fear, and loneliness. For a time, nothing makes sense. Whatever you had assumed was the case, wasn't true. Whoever you thought loved you, didn't. And there is nothing at all you can do about it.

Being lied to, led on, rejected, can lead to such a fear of abandonment that you put up physical or emotional walls. They may be the only way to keep safe from future threats. Or like me, you might take it to the ultimate level—the fear of attachment. You feel so burned by the world that you detach on every level. For me it was a terribly dark place to be and eventually I was left with two options: to either fix my broken heart or die of it.

If you too are emotionally broken, be reassured: it is possible to heal. And the first step is to listen to your heart. That means acknowledging the pain. It may sound obvious to have to acknowledge something that can feel like it's killing you from within, but it's only through listening to your heart that you can start the healing process. Know that everybody hurts sometimes, but no one has to hurt forever.

"I have found the paradox, that if you love until it hurts, there can be no more hurt, only more love." ~ Mother Teresa

Healing Hurt: A letter to your broken heart

Write a letter to your broken heart. Ask those questions to which there are difficult answers— why me? how did it happen? why did they do it? what's going to happen to me in the future? Let the negativity and emotions flow. This is for your eyes only, so don't hold back. Write freely and let it all out. Acknowledge your pain.

Then look at what you've written and make the decision that today is the start of a new beginning. Tell yourself that you're going to mend your brokenness and learn to love again.

"Let no one who loves be called altogether unhappy. Even love unreturned has its rainbow." ~ J. M. Barrie

Chapter 2:
A Soft Place to Fall

"Numbing the pain for a while will make it worse when you finally feel it." ~ J. K. Rowling

When brokenness is all that you have, there's little choice but to pick up the pieces and start again. As you do, you'll need a soft place to fall. Managing the pain is a journey through vulnerability and despair to strength and hope. Heartbreak is complicated and there's no easy solution, but as you take steps to take care of yourself, you take the first steps to restoring your heart.

When something is causing us pain, it's natural to want it to end. Running away from, or blocking, the pain might feel effective in the short term, but in the long run it will reappear, with the possibility that the damage will have become greater. From that there may be little or no escape.

I didn't realize just how much pain I was in until I found something I thought could take it all away. Unfortunately, my relief came in the form of alcohol. From my first taste of alcohol as a teenager I was hooked. Unaware of the power of alcohol and the dangers of self-medicating, I drank to numb the pain of the past, to give me the confidence to manage each day, and to take away my fears of the future.

Self-medicating can be very dangerous. Alcohol, drugs, food, other relationships— anything that you use to numb or avoid pain should be used with caution. Going out for a night out and forgetting your troubles for a while is fine, but if you're seeking to do this all the time, beware. Don't numb the pain, find the courage to heal.

"Sometimes our first and greatest dare is asking for support." ~ Brené Brown

One of the greatest challenges I faced when I started on my journey to recovery was allowing other people to nurture, comfort, and guide me. For me, asking for support meant I was a complete failure as a human being. But how wrong I was! In fact I learned that by reaching out, not only did I find the way to move on from my past insecurities, but I also gained courage and strength in the process.

Mourn your loss at your own pace and treat yourself with the same compassion you would treat someone else in pain. Keep putting one foot in front of the other as you move from your darkest despair into the light of hope. Just as love hurts, so too does it heal.

Now is the time to take care of yourself. When times are hard make sure you surround yourself with those who will care for and nurture you, inspire and encourage you. If you've experienced rejection you may feel wary of trusting anyone, but the wall you build as a safeguard is the same wall that will, in turn, isolate and imprison you. Allow others to be part of your soft place to fall.

"All healing is first a healing of the heart." ~ Carl Townsend

There was a point in my life when I felt I had been so hurt by others that I couldn't envisage trusting, let alone loving, anyone ever again. But living in that state of brokenness was like being in an emotional prison. I was resigning myself to a life sentence of nursing old wounds.

The trepidation of attachment made me put up the barriers of mistrust and hostility. I alternated between thinking, *I'm never going to let anyone near me ever again,* to *I'm going to hurt them before they hurt me.* Relentless self-pity kept me trapped in a vicious cycle of hopelessness.

My turning point was the realization that life goes on. I could choose to stay with the pain of the past or rise above it. There were days when I thought my tears would never stop and the heartache would never ease. But it was only through experiencing my vulnerability that I could be emotionally restored.

Finding your soft place to fall means getting up when you're down and finding your smile again after the tears. It means managing the pain and telling yourself, *As long as I have a heart I can heal. And as long as I can heal I have a heart.*

> *"I will soothe you and heal you,*
> *I will bring you roses.*
> *I too have been covered with thorns."* ~ Rumi

Healing Hurt: Create your soft place to fall

Write a list of everything you think could help you through your transition from pain to peace. Find ways to be kind to yourself, both physically and mentally. Make time to pray and meditate. Faith can be the source not only of comfort but of hope. Or resolve to have a time of serenity each day: close your eyes and relax. Think about who could support you, or who could support you more. Don't be afraid to reach out to others. Those that love you will love you through both the good times and the bad.

"Smile, breathe and go slowly." ~ Thich Nhat Hanh

but when you come to a place where you accept the ending, you'll also come to the door of your new beginning. Allow serenity to take your mind, body, and soul from a place of pain to a place of peace.

"Acceptance looks like a passive state, but in reality it brings something entirely new into this world. That peace, a subtle energy vibration, is consciousness." ~ Eckhart Tolle

Healing Hurt: Seek your serenity

A broken heart can cause chaos in your mind. Tranquility will quieten it. Set aside some time each day to reflect, pray, or meditate. Whether it's the "Serenity Prayer" or a favorite verse or quote, allow the calmness of the words to filter down from your head to your heart.

"Every breath we take, every step we take, can be filled with joy, peace, and serenity." ~ Thich Nhat Hanh

Chapter 4:
The Freedom of Forgiveness

"Forgiveness is an act of the will, and the will can function regardless of the temperature of the heart." ~ Corrie ten Boom

"I'll never forgive you." Said in the heat of the moment it can feel like you really mean it. You've been hurt. The pain is unbearable. You'll never forget and you'll never forgive. End of story.

Except that it's not. Not wanting to forgive—or not being able to—brings further anguish. It doesn't diminish over time like memories can. It can filter into your soul, filling you with bitterness and intolerance. Thoughts of revenge will trap you in the very past that you despise and keep your heart like stone. Just as healing is a process that occurs over time, so too is forgiveness. Whatever your situation, however deep your pain, forgiveness is essential to your healing.

In my own life, one of the main barriers that prevented my emotional recovery from childhood trauma was not being able to forgive my parents. Until I found a way to forgive them, I kept hold of the anger and pain, I continued looking for something to numb me from reality, I carried on thinking that life owed me. It didn't.

One of the most difficult experiences I've been through in my life was ending the non-existent relationship I had with my mother. I had no other choice but to allow myself to grieve for the woman I remembered, for the mother that should have been.

Eventually only the need to forgive remained. And with time and tears I came to a place of mercy and compassion. I didn't do it for her, I did it for me, so that I could finish with a part of my life that had caused me so much emotional pain and physical destruction.

Forgiveness released me from the torment of longing to know *why*? Once my mother no longer existed in my heart or my mind, neither did the need to fill in the past. It had been over for my mother many years ago, but finally it was over for me too.

"We think that forgiveness is weakness, but it's absolutely not; it takes a very strong person to forgive." ~ T. D. Jakes

There have been other instances when I have been lied to or let down by people I trusted, respected, or loved. Each time I've had to make the choice to forgive. Even when every fiber in my body has screamed *Never!*, I've still resolved to make my peace. You can make that same choice too.

I've come to embrace the importance of forgiveness, not simply because it sets me free, but because it's the right thing to do. But there is a difference between being compassionate and being spineless, between being forgiving and being used. Remember, forgiveness is not to be confused with being a doormat or allowing the offender to get away with it. Nor does it mean you shouldn't express your grief and upset. It means that you're willing to move beyond your rawness and vulnerability, and that you're willing to let go of the negativity and animosity which hold you emotionally hostage.

Forgiveness is not a form of acceptance or surrender, it's a battle cry. Another person's actions have already stolen enough from you; you can refuse to let them take any more. Even if they don't acknowledge their wrongdoing or offer an apology, by forgiving them you're taking control of a situation over which you had none.

"You can't forgive without loving. And I don't mean sentimentality. I don't mean mush. I mean having enough courage to stand up and say, 'I forgive. I'm finished with it'." ~ Maya Angelou

Losing someone can make you feel very angry. Even if they were ill and it wasn't their fault, it's natural to have feelings of anger and resentment towards them. Their life has impacted on yours and you're left alone. Or if someone has betrayed you, their words and actions can continuously replay in your mind, leaving you depressed, frustrated, and emotionally exhausted. Yet forgiveness has the power to release you from your torment, whatever the circumstances.

If the other person was in the wrong but you're hoping to restore the relationship, you may have to make a decision to be the hero. This means seeing past the offense and choosing to let go. It means acknowledging that you hate what they did to you, but are willing to forgive. You can choose to be bigger than the resentment, the anger, and the fear. And you deserve to be free from any more pain.

By forgiving you are not condoning what someone else has done or said; you're not being weak. Rather you're revealing your strength, for it's easier to stay angry than to dig deep into your reserves of understanding. And the sooner you forgive, the sooner you empower yourself to heal. Reclaiming your spirit of compassion will set your mind, body, and soul free to move to your place of peace. Now that's the freedom of forgiveness!

"To forgive is to set a prisoner free and discover that the prisoner was you." ~ Lewis B. Smedes

Healing Hurt: A letter of forgiveness

It takes time to overcome an offense. Allow your heart to soften by writing a letter of forgiveness to the person who has offended you. Don't send it; simply write it and read it back to yourself. Your head may give you plenty of reasons not to forgive, but remember—this is about you, not them. You're letting go of bitterness and pain. You're embracing forgiveness and peace.

"Forgiveness is not an occasional act. It is a permanent attitude." ~ Martin Luther King

Chapter 5:
The Gift of Gratitude

"Acknowledging the good that you already have in your life is the foundation for all abundance." ~ Eckhart Tolle

It may seem odd to think about being thankful when you're in pain, but gratitude is a great soother for the heart. When you're in the initial throes of a broken heart, it can truly feel like the whole of your life is in ruins. All you know is that everything is a mess and life has fallen apart.

No matter how agonizing your situation, there's always something to be grateful for. After a tragic death, you might feel grateful for the person's life and the legacy they left. If it's a relationship you've lost, you can be thankful for the friends and other relationships that are still there to nurture and support you. If you've been betrayed by someone, all the more reason to appreciate those people you can trust.

If you're too raw to turn to people, then turn to nature: watch a beautiful sunset, take a walk in the forest, stroke a loving pet. Or draw inspiration from the world around you: find something to laugh about, turn on some good music, dance till you drop. It might sound clichéd, but it doesn't matter as long as you're doing something that offers gentle relief.

And if you're still struggling, then just remember that you're alive. If you think that's the *only* thing you have to be grateful for, that's okay—there are graveyards full of people who'd swap places with you, even if only for a day.

When you struggle with adversity it can be tempting to look at others and envy them. Some people appear to glide through life untroubled and totally blessed. But that's merely a perception. No one gets through life without trials; everyone has their battles to fight. You're definitely not alone in your despair.

So during those times when the pain is ripping you apart, dig deep into your soul and search for the things you can still be grateful for. When your wounded heart is screaming for attention, don't focus on what you have lost, but on what you *have* — and be thankful for it.

"If you are not living in Joy, you are out of integrity with your Soul." ~ Michael Bernard Beckwith

Consider thankfulness as an opening to hope and joy, both of which are within your grasp and which form the foundations for a contented soul and peaceful heart. Happiness is all about you, but only you can make yourself happy. So if you're relying on somebody else to make you feel valued and loved, think again.

While a loving relationship involves caring for another and meeting each other's needs, it's not anyone else's responsibility to keep you "fixed." True happiness lies within your authentic self and is revealed through your heart and soul. Only you have the keys to your heart and only you can open the window to your soul.

"Happiness is when what you think, what you say, and what you do are in harmony." ~ Mahatma Gandhi

One of the most important lessons I've learned on my own journey of healing is that joyful living is a choice. Even though you can't change yesterday, or control what happens today, or prevent what tomorrow may bring, you can choose to accept your past, be thankful for each day, and embrace the future. These choices can bring you to a place of joy.

For me, the joy in my life comes from knowing that I may not have what I want, but I do have what I need. Self-worth, sobriety, and a sense of belonging also contribute to my happiness. And each day is made complete by a faith that heals and renews, by the love of my family, and by the companionship of friends. And I'm grateful for them all.

The gift of gratitude is joy. So give yourself permission to embrace thankfulness and happiness despite your pain, and allow them both to bring you to a place of emotional restoration.

"Be content with what you have; rejoice in the way things are. When you realize there is nothing lacking, the whole world belongs to you." ~ Lao Tzu

Healing Hurt: A letter of gratitude

It may feel that in losing your loved one you have lost it all. The void can feel vast. So now is the time to remind yourself not of what you don't have, but of what you *do* have. Write a letter of gratitude for everything and everyone you *have* in your life. Focus on the little things and allow them to become the big things in your life.

"He is a wise man who does not grieve for the things which he has not, but rejoices for those which he has." ~ Epictetus

Chapter 6:
Alone Doesn't Have to Be Lonely

"Loneliness is the poverty of self; solitude is the richness of self."
~ May Sarton

Loving someone and being loved back is wonderful until that love is no longer there. If your life as a couple has come to an end as a result of the other person's decision, it's the sense of rejection that can cause the deepest hurt. And if your love is rejected as a result of betrayal, the pain can be agonizing.

Where once you knew that you were the only one, you now know that there is someone else. But true love can't be shared. The love that that person had for you was too precious, too deep, and too tender to be passed on. Yet someone else is now receiving the love you believed to be yours. From the moment you become aware of the betrayal, so begins the incessant and intense ache in your heart, and an overwhelming loneliness.

"Loneliness is never more cruel than when it is felt in close propinquity with someone who has ceased to communicate."
~ Germaine Greer

Both emotional betrayal and physical infidelity are deal-breakers in a loving relationship. When the man I loved betrayed me, I tried at first to pretend he hadn't. I refused to consider that his other relationship was anything more than friendship. Of course, this was exactly how he justified his actions: he was simply offering support and consolation to someone who had been through a difficult time. So who was I to be challenging such kind words and offers of help?

I tried hard to convince myself that he was innocent, yet deep down I knew differently. In matters of the heart, a woman's intuition is rarely mistaken. Actually I'd known right from the start: he exaggerated how he disliked her while his body language indicated the opposite; he made not-so-subtle comments about her stunning looks and amazing figure, which, when repeated back to him, he dismissed as a joke; he made special efforts to look nice in her company and was the first to volunteer if she needed a lift. Goodness, I saw it all!

And I heard it all too: soothing words to reassure her in her time of need; tender offers of assistance day or night; nothing was too much trouble. Then inevitably the words I least wanted to hear were declared to her with passion: "I love you." It was at that point I realized I had never felt so lonely — and that the only option was to be alone.

"Remember that although the distinction can be difficult to draw, loneliness and solitude are different." ~ Gretchen Rubin

When a relationship ends it can take time to readjust. You may not enjoy being alone but you can learn to love your own company. Resolve to stop reminiscing about what it was like when you were part of a couple and celebrate your singleness. Without another person to consider, make compromises with, or look out for, you can do what you want, when you want. Embrace your free spirit, rediscover those things you used to love doing and enjoy a new you.

Be patient with yourself and don't rebound into another relationship until you're comfortable with being on your own. If you take a broken heart filled with neediness into a new relationship, it will break that relationship too. Wait until you're whole, then you'll be able to give yourself wholly.

"I never found a companion that was so companionable as solitude." ~ Henry David Thoreau

Through my own journey of healing I've discovered that as much as I appreciate being around others, I also enjoy my own company. Instead of trying to shut out my own voice, I embraced *who* I was and *what* I was. And it was through this process that I found I could be just as fulfilled and contented on my own as when I was in a relationship.

In fact, the more I healed from being part of a couple, the more open I became to new relationships and the less time I spent on my own. Today, I'm in the wonderful position of being filled with faith and surrounded by friends and family who bring me contentment and joy on many levels. Yet I'm not dependent on them to assuage any emptiness.

I'm now in that privileged place of being able to say that I don't feel lonely. For me, being alone means to be at peace with myself. And for anyone who has stayed in a relationship rather than be single, they'll know that this is a gift. Yet it's a gift you can claim simply by learning to love yourself, for when you do, alone doesn't have to be lonely.

"You cannot be lonely if you like the person you're alone with."
~ Wayne Dyer

Healing Hurt: Embracing solitude

If you've been used to living your life as part of a couple, then singleness can be difficult to accept. But it is possible to learn to enjoy your own company. Dive into your solitude and heal your heart from within. Make a list of all the things you can now do because you're single and start doing them. Embrace the freedom of being able to make YOU a priority.

"How wrong it is for a woman to expect the man to build the world she wants, rather than to create it herself." ~ Anaïs Nin

Chapter 7:
Love Yourself

"We are what we believe we are." ~ Benjamin N. Cardozo

I spent many years battling the depression and addiction that defined my existence. But while rejection and abuse had a huge impact on how I felt, the fundamental issue was that I didn't *like* myself, let alone *love* myself.

Outwardly I wore the mask of the independent, capable, confident woman, but underneath I was lonely, confused, and broken. Most of all, I was ashamed of who I was. At the lowest point of my life I was a chronically depressed alcoholic who had lost everything. By society's standards I was a complete failure. Somehow everyone else seemed to have a life that I could only dream of and the love I longed for. I thought I could have neither because I wasn't good enough.

"No one can make you feel inferior without your consent."
~ Eleanor Roosevelt

I lived my life as a victim because I allowed other people to define me. Realizing this was a breakthrough moment in my life. After a lifetime of hearing and believing the worst about myself, it wasn't easy to make the transition to cultivating a positive self-image and believing that I deserved good things in my life.

Occasionally my past does creep back into my thoughts, and sometimes I face criticisms and rejections, but I no longer internalize them and wear them as a label. Today I know I am loved, trusted, and respected by the people who matter to me. And I love, trust, and respect myself.

"I long, as does every human being, to be at home wherever I find myself." ~ Maya Angelou.

If you are struggling to love yourself, make a decision to challenge some of those labels that you think define you and start loving yourself for who you are. You can't change what someone has said to you, but you can change how you respond to it. Love yourself enough to stop taking on board the bad and start absorbing the good. Stop believing you can't and start believing that you can.

If you learn to change how you think of yourself, others will change how they see you. The person you thought you were will become a memory and the *real* you will have a chance to shine. You may feel inadequate, vulnerable, and unlovable, but as you let go of past hurts you'll be able to allow your wonderful authentic self to emerge.

Loving yourself is reassurance that you're okay, even when everything and everyone around you is falling apart or in turmoil. It's accepting that you don't have to be perfect, that your imperfections are part of your uniqueness. It's being at home with yourself, wherever you are.

"What lies behind us and what lies before us are tiny matters compared to what lies within us." ~ Ralph Waldo Emerson

Healing Hurt: Lists of love

As clichéd as it sounds, life is short a
precious to be wasted wishing you
somewhere else. Write a list of everyth
yourself. Describe what you like about yourself phy
Commend your talents and abilities; celebrate your
personality traits. Then write another list of everything
you love about your life. Define the good points from past
and present on every level—practical, social, physical,
emotional, spiritual.

Pick one item from each list and use them as
affirmations: "I love myself because _____"; "I love my
life because_____".

"Your time is limited, so don't waste it living someone else's life."
~ Steve Jobs

Chapter 8:
Letting Go

"The past has no power to stop you from being present now. Only your grievance about the past can do that. What is grievance? The baggage of old thought and emotion." ~ Lao Tzu

When you've suffered disappointments and been left heart-broken by loved ones it can be hard to move on. The shock, denial, guilt, or anger you experience as a part of grieving are natural for a time. Yet if you don't progress past those stages, it's all too easy to become trapped in the past.

Life is about living in the present and anticipating the future. But you can't do that if you're carrying the baggage of yesterday into today, and when further difficulties arise they simply add to your luggage of psychological pain. It gets heavier and you become encumbered. Instead of embracing each day afresh, you return to the familiar mental battleground. You replay the same scenarios or repeat the same negative thoughts, only to be hurt all over again. Your bags are stuffed with rejection, shame, bitterness, jealousy, mistrust, apathy, confusion, anger, fear. They can be filled to the top, but it doesn't matter — you find another bag and carry that too.

"Live so you do not have to look back and say: 'God, how I have wasted my life'." ~ Elisabeth Kübler-Ross

rying the baggage of my childhood
abuse. I carried them for so long that
ırt of me. Wherever I went those bags
:ause the loss of my mother and abuse by
my father wᴇɪᴄ ᴀ.ɪ I had to define me.

Instead of using those traumas as steppingstones to a better tomorrow, I used them to build a prison wall. Instead of taking each day as an opportunity to restore and renew, I added to my pain. Instead of living my life as the person I wanted to be, I lived it as a victim of my past. It's not really surprising, then, that depression and alcoholism became my coping strategies to help me carry my emotional load, and that relationships were doomed to fail before they had even begun.

Like many who have gone through life clutching on to the baggage of trauma or tragedy, I eventually saw the damage that was being caused physically and emotionally. However, not only did I not know how to let go, I wasn't sure that I wanted to—the prospect of change was so terrifying.

I'd carried my broken heart with me for so long that I couldn't imagine being without it. Fear of change kept me locked in the familiarity of my existence—even if it was a sad and broken existence. Everything defined me as a victim and a failure, and as I finally crumbled under the pressure of my past, I knew that I had to make the choice to give up or get up.

"Come to me, all you who are weary and burdened, and I will give you rest." ~ Matthew 11:28–30

It wasn't easy. I gave myself permission to hand over everything that was harming me. Gradually, over time, I released all the pain and fought the demons that had troubled me for as long as I could remember. Faith taught me that I didn't have to understand why I'd endured such trials and that there was nothing I could do to change the past.

Acceptance of what had gone before helped me to begin living in the present and start looking to the future. Then forgiveness provided the key to set me free to clear out all the baggage. With my load lightened, I found gratitude for my life and vowed to continue my journey of healing.

Now I have a faith-filled heart full of hope, love, joy, and trust. I continue my journey in sobriety with gratitude and serenity. No longer burdened by yesterday, I choose to appreciate today, whatever it brings, and eagerly await tomorrow.

Take a look at the baggage you're carrying around with you today. Whatever the burdens in your heart— bitterness and resentment, rejection and loneliness, worry and fear—you can decide to lay them down. You may have had no control over what happened to you in the past, but you do have a choice as to what happens now. You can choose to lay down the past. You can choose to accept and forgive. You can choose to heal your heart and find peace for your soul.

"Vulnerability is the birthplace of innovation, creativity and change." ~ Brené Brown

As I traveled along my journey to emotional healing I discovered that my vulnerability was no longer my weakness, it was a revelation of my authentic self. No longer confined by my past or defined by others, I found the courage to heal and the freedom to recreate myself as the person I was meant to be.

And that is what I would wish for you. Don't let the events of the past keep you from enjoying the future that awaits you. Put down those bags crammed with the destructive negativity of failed relationships or lost love. Leave them and don't look back. You don't need those things any more.

It's time to find some bright new vibrant luggage and fill it with everything that can heal your mind, body, and soul. The things that nurture and uplift are weightless. Convince yourself that now is the time to start traveling light.

"Letting go means to come to the realization that some people are a part of your history, but not a part of your destiny." ~ Steve Maraboli

Healing Hurt: Say goodbye to the pain of the past

Write a letter to your inner child. Be gentle and nurturing. Encourage that broken soul to let go of all that is painful from the past and all that is harmful in the present. Don't hold back. Then encourage your inner child to reclaim a life filled with good things that will heal and inspire.

"We must be willing to let go of the life we've planned, so as to have the life that is waiting for us." ~ Joseph Campbell

Chapter 9:
Finding Your Passion

"Whatever you think you can do or believe you can do, begin it. Action has magic, grace and power in it." ~ Goethe

It's over. You are letting go of the past and you're making good progress on your journey to heal. The rawness has gone, the scars are forming, and you can finally breathe again, laugh again, love again. It's time to find your pathway to passion.

Our passions as an adult often start with our inner child, so it's important that your inner child is respected and nurtured, ready to release your authentic and creative aspirations. Be aware that a damaged child needs to be healed to the point where the wounds of the past cannot open, for a broken soul will build broken dreams.

If you were abused as a child you may not have had the opportunity to dream. Fear-filled days of keeping the peace and holding on to the silence took up all your emotional energy. It's hard to have a passion for life when your life isn't in your hands. But today you can reclaim that life and dream the dream.

As the victim of an abusive partnership, and as the narcissist in your life gradually made everyday existence all about them, you may well have abandoned your own pathway to personal freedom. When you live in an environment where you're criticized for everything and made to believe you are nothing, there's no point in thinking of personal desires. But now you're free to recover those desires and follow your heart.

Maybe life has just thrown up crisis after crisis and you've been left feeling defeated and overwhelmed. Or you're dealing with chronic illness and pain. It may seem pointless to pursue notions that you can't envisage when everyday challenges take up all your time and energy. But there *is* a point. Passion for the future is a great healer of pain in the present.

"The greatest danger for most of us is not that our aim is too high and we miss it, but that it is too low and we reach it."
~ Ken Robinson

Your pathway to passion can be as big or as small as you choose. It can spring from hopes of yesteryear or from an epiphany of today. What matters is that you find that zest, that energy, that longing, for something that reflects your authentic self, and that you pursue it boldly.

Be brave and let the spark ignite the dreams that have lain dormant. Search your unconscious for those hidden aspirations and bring them into reality. Be confident and creative in your thinking, and visualize your future. Embrace the fear of change and use it to fuel the excitement and anticipation of the good things to come.

True happiness is living authentically, so remind yourself that you are an exceptional and precious individual who deserves a good life. Don't waste time and energy trying to be someone you're not, for it'll only lead to discontentment and discouragement. Similarly, forget about those things you can't do and focus on what you can. Most importantly, make your passion your purpose.

"Shoot for the moon. Even if you miss you will land among stars."
~ Les Brown

A childhood of being repeatedly reminded that I was worthless, ugly, fat, and inadequate in every way laid the foundations for me to become just that as an adult. I never loved myself and couldn't imagine anyone truly loving me. There was no point having dreams because they would be crushed. There was no point having goals because they would never be realized. There was no point trying to accomplish anything because I was a failure. There was no point looking for love because I was unlovable.

Life is tough for everyone at different times, but it's your response to challenges that sets you apart. You don't have to beat yourself up when things don't go according to plan. You don't have to give up because the moon is further away than you thought and it's harder to reach than you ever imagined.

Instead, you can determine to enjoy the ride, bumps and all. And you can use the hardships and heartaches as platforms for learning and growing. Keep your moon in sight and look around for some stars to use as steppingstones to your destination. Remember, a breakdown can be the experience that broke you or that helped *you* break through.

"May the passion to be all that God wants you to be sweep across your soul like a gentle breeze." ~ T. D. Jakes

For me, passion and purpose are meaningless unless I have faith, for faith not only reassures me but fills me with expectations of what can be achieved. With the belief that the possibilities are endless, that the impossible can be made possible, life becomes a journey filled with aspirations and hope.

Whatever your spiritual convictions, dare to dream that there's something greater than you wanting the best for you. Use your intuition to find and follow your heart's desires. Reach into your unconscious and become consciously inspired.

"The future belongs to those who believe in the beauty of their dreams." ~ Eleanor Roosevelt

Don't be discouraged with setbacks or despair if others don't share your vision and enthusiasm. You're not dependent on the approval of others who may feel threatened, jealous, or fearful of your potential and success. It's your life. It's your path.

Remind yourself that passion will keep burning as long as you have that spark of desire and that spirit of commitment. Not every vision has to be a huge life-changing event. Little steps are just as significant. Big or small, it's never too late to dream.

Once you're able to love yourself, you can believe that not only does life have a purpose, but that you have a right to pursue your passions. As your heart heals so your

capacity to dream emerges. So star
unimaginable, reach for the unattain
impossible.

"Let the beauty of what you love be what you do." ~ Rum...

Healing Hurt: A passionate heart

Write a letter to your authentic self, describing your
passions and purpose in life. Be bold and think outside the
box as you include your hopes and dreams. There are no
boundaries; the outcomes can be endless. Then describe
how you can fulfill your purpose and share your
passionate heart. Be brave and take action. Follow your
dreams.

*"Without leaps of imagination, or dreaming, we lose the
excitement of possibilities. Dreaming, after all, is a form of
planning." ~ Gloria Steinem*

Chapter 10:
The Meaning of Love

"There is only one happiness in life, to love and be loved."
~ George Sand

Love is a word that's seen and heard everywhere. It's used freely to describe emotions and feelings. It conjures up romantic notions and lust. Yet there's so much more to love than just a sentiment that makes you feel good.

Of course it's wonderful to make people feel wanted and needed through words that are encouraging or compassionate. But when you use the words "I love you", it can take the relationship to a completely different level. Those three little words aren't just a statement of affection or admiration, they can be the ultimate declaration of attachment and loyalty.

When you tell someone you love them you are investing your heart, mind, and soul in them. "I love you" should never be said lightly. Those words are both precious and powerful.

"Love is patient, love is kind. It does not envy, it does not boast, it is not proud. It does not dishonor others, it is not self-seeking, it is not easily angered, it keeps no record of wrongs. Love does not delight in evil but rejoices with the truth. It always protects, always trusts, always hopes, always perseveres."
~ Corinthians 13:4–8

As well as needing to be loved, we need to love others. For me, this means not just speaking of love, but showing it. Gifts, tokens of generosity, or sensual actions are all ways to demonstrate love, but just as important are respect, empathy, commitment, and authenticity. In that context, "I love you" has huge impact and meaning.

In my own journey of healing, I found it was in my moments of greatest despair that the light of my faith shone the brightest. It provided me with the strength, comfort, and gratitude that I needed to affirm my worthiness. And it reminded me that as broken as I was, I was lovable and precious, that my heart could be restored.

It wasn't easy. I had to learn to look at myself and say "I love you" before I could declare it to anyone else. Even now, I'm much more at ease at telling those I care for that I love them than saying it to myself. But the reality is that you can't give away what you don't have, and that includes love.

"Being deeply loved by someone gives you strength, while loving someone deeply gives you courage." ~ Lao Tzu

When you've been hurt in the past it's easy to vow that you'll never love again, but heartache and heartbreak are part of life's trials. Even if you feel love has lost its meaning for ever, it hasn't. The antidote for pain is love. Just as love hurts, so does it heal. In the rawness of an ending of something you believed to be special, it can feel like your heart is broken beyond repair. But it *is* possible to recover, and to discover a love so infinite and complete that the pain of the past is but a wisp of memory.

That same love you gave away must now be used in abundance to nurture your mind, body, and soul. Stop telling yourself that you'll never love anyone again. You will—but only when you completely and unconditionally immerse yourself in the love that lies within.

Your new life and your new love await. Join me by resolving to be stronger than the pain of yesterday, find peace for today, and pursue your dreams for tomorrow. My broken heart has healed, and so can yours.

"Love one another." ~ John 13:34

Healing Hurt: Letter to your new love

Write a letter to your next love. You don't have to have found a new love yet; simply imagine who it is and tell them why you love them. Reflect on your letter. What does it tell you about what you're looking for in your next love?

"The love you seek is seeking you at this moment."
~ Deepak Chopra

Inspirational Quotations for Each Day of the Year

A collection of inspirational quotations, reflective thoughts and empowering aspirations to help you live your life as the person you were meant to be.

January: Love Yourself

1. *Within you, you will find everything you need to be complete.* ~ Bryant McGill

2. *Your past doesn't have to define your present.* ~ The Hurt Healer

3. *Too many people overvalue what they are not and undervalue what they are.* ~ Malcolm S. Forbes

4. *Vulnerability is the birthplace of innovation, creativity, and change.* ~ Brené Brown

5. *Between stimulus and response there is a space. In that space is our power to choose our response. In our response lies our growth and our freedom.* ~ Viktor E. Frankl

6. *There is nothing noble about being superior to some other man. The true nobility is in being superior to your previous self.* ~ Hindu Proverb

7. *You don't have to be perfect; your imperfections are part of your uniqueness.* ~ The Hurt Healer

8. *I am fearfully and wonderfully made.* ~ Psalm 139:14

9. *You will be a beautiful person, as long as you see the beauty in others.* ~ Bryant McGill

10. *When you recover or discover something that nourishes your soul and brings joy, care enough about yourself to make room for it in your life.*
~ Jean Shinoda Bolen

11. *As I traveled along my journey to recovery I discovered that my vulnerability was no longer my weakness, it was a revelation of my authentic self.* ~ The Hurt Healer

12. *Individuality is only possible if it unfolds from wholeness.* ~ David Bohm

13. *It is never too late to be what you might have been.* ~ George Eliot

14. *Whatever is stopping you from loving yourself, caring for yourself, being yourself, let it go.*
~ The Hurt Healer

15. *You cannot be lonely if you like the person you're alone with.* ~ Wayne Dyer

16. *Who looks outside, dreams; who looks inside, awakes.* ~ Carl Jung

17. *You either teach people to treat you with dignity and respect, or you don't.* ~ Dr. Phil McGraw

18. *If loving someone else means you have to stop loving yourself that is too high a price to pay.*
~ The Hurt Healer

19. *Love is the great miracle cure. Loving ourselves works miracles in our lives.* ~ Louise L. Hay

20. *Something inside you emerges ... an innate, indwelling peace, stillness, aliveness. It is the unconditioned, who you are in your essence. It is what you had been looking for in the love object. It is yourself.* ~ Eckhart Tolle

21. *The snow goose need not bathe to make itself white. Neither need you do anything but be yourself.*
~ Lao Tzu

22. *What lies behind us and what lies before us are tiny matters compared to what lies within us.*
~ Ralph Waldo Emerson

23. *The most powerful relationship you will ever have is the relationship with yourself.* ~ Steve Maraboli

24. *Plant your own garden and decorate your own soul, instead of waiting for someone to bring you flowers.*
~ Veronica A. Shoffstall

25. *How people treat you is their karma; how you react is yours.* ~ Wayne Dyer

26. *You yourself, as much as anybody in the entire universe, deserve your love and affection.*
~ Buddha

27. *Love is but the discovery of ourselves in others, and the delight in the recognition.* ~ Alexander Smith

28. *Be yourself; everyone else is already taken.*
~ Oscar Wilde

29. *Your task is not to seek for Love, but merely to seek and find all the barriers within yourself that you have built up against it.* ~ Rumi

30. *You are unique, and if that is not fulfilled, then something has been lost.* ~ Martha Graham

31. *We delight in the beauty of the butterfly, but rarely admit the changes it has gone through to achieve that beauty.* ~ Maya Angelou

February: Love

1. *Love is the beauty of the soul.* ~ Saint Augustine

2. *It's not how much we give but how much love we put into giving.* ~ Mother Teresa

3. *Love is the antidote to pain.* ~ The Hurt Healer

4. *A new command I give you: love one another. As I have loved you, so you must love one another.* ~ John 13:34

5. *A flower cannot blossom without sunshine, and man cannot live without love.* ~ Max Müller

6. *Love is patient, love is kind. It does not envy, it does not boast, it is not proud. It does not dishonor others, it is not self-seeking, it is not easily angered, it keeps no record of wrongs. Love does not delight in evil but rejoices with the truth. It always protects, always trusts, always hopes, always perseveres.* ~ Corinthians 13:4–8

7. *True love stories never have endings.* ~ Richard Bach

8. *Trust your heart if the seas catch fire, live by love though the stars walk backward.* ~ E. E. Cummings

9. *Love is a better teacher than duty.* ~ Albert Einstein

10. *Being deeply loved by someone gives you strength, while loving someone deeply gives you courage.* ~ Lao Tzu

11. *For where your treasure is, there your heart will be also.*
    ~ Matthew 6:21

12. *The love you seek is seeking you at this moment.*
    ~ Deepak Chopra

13. *Love is a canvas furnished by nature and embroidered by imagination.* ~ Voltaire

14. *I have found the paradox, that if you love until it hurts, there can be no more hurt, only more love.*
    ~ Mother Teresa

15. *We waste time looking for the perfect lover, instead of creating the perfect love.* ~ Tom Robbins

16. *Life is the flower for which love is the honey.*
    ~ Victor Hugo

17. *Hatred does not cease by hatred, but only by love; this is the eternal rule.* ~ Buddha

18. *Let the beauty of what you love be what you do.*
    ~ Rumi

19. *One is loved because one is loved. No reason is needed for loving.* ~ Paulo Coelho

20. *Above all, love each other deeply, because love covers over a multitude of sins.* ~ 1 Peter 4:8

21. *Immature love says: "I love you because I need you." Mature love says "I need you because I love you."*
    ~ Erich Fromm

22. *You have within you more love than you can ever understand.* ~ Rumi

23. *Though lovers be lost love shall not.* ~ Dylan Thomas

24. *Love … it surrounds every being and extends slowly to embrace all that shall be.* ~ Khalil Gibran

25. *Ultimately love is everything.* ~ M. Scott Peck

26. *If equal affection cannot be, Let the more loving one be me.* ~ W. H. Auden

27. *Stop telling yourself that you will never love anyone again. You will.* ~ The Hurt Healer

28. *There is only one happiness in life, to love and be loved.* ~ George Sand

If it's a Leap Year:
29. *Love's greatest gift is its ability to make everything it touches sacred.* ~ Barbara De Angelis

March: Kindness

1. *I've learned that people will forget what you said, people will forget what you did, but people will never forget how you made them feel.* ~ Maya Angelou

2. *Act with kindness, but do not expect gratitude.* ~ Confucius

3. *Truth is a deep kindness that teaches us to be content in our everyday life and share with the people the same happiness.* ~ Khalil Gibran

4. *Be kind and compassionate to one another, forgiving each other, just as in Christ God forgave you.* ~ Ephesians 4:32

5. *Try to be a rainbow in someone's cloud.* ~ Maya Angelou

6. *Whether it's faith, family, friends or from inside your soul, it's always good to have a soft place to fall.* ~ The Hurt Healer

7. *The only way to tell the truth is to speak with kindness. Only the words of a loving man can be heard.* ~ Henry David Thoreau

8. *Do not let kindness and truth leave you. Bind them around your neck, write them on the tablet of your heart.* ~ Proverbs 3:3

9. *Be kind whenever possible. It is always possible.* ~ Dalai Lama

10. *Be the change that you wish to see in the world.* ~ Mahatma Gandhi

11. *Tear out arrogance and seed humility. Exchange love for hate – thereby, making the present comfortable and the future promising.* ~ Maya Angelou

12. *Your life does not get better by chance, it gets better by change.* ~ Jim Rohn

13. *Write injuries in sand, kindnesses in marble.* ~ French proverb

14. *Giving connects two people, the giver and the receiver, and this connection gives birth to a new sense of belonging.* ~ Deepak Chopra

15. *Those who bring sunshine into the lives of others, cannot keep it from themselves.* ~ J. M. Barrie

16. *When we feel love and kindness toward others, it not only makes others feel loved and cared for, but it helps us also to develop inner happiness and peace.* ~ Dalai Lama

17. *Just as to reap good crops you have to sow your seed in good soil, you have to sow your love into a good relationship.* ~ The Hurt Healer

18. *Lord, make me an instrument of thy peace. Where there is hatred, let me sow love.* ~ Francis of Assisi

19. *Affection is responsible for nine-tenths of whatever solid and durable happiness there is in our lives.* ~ C. S. Lewis

20. *But the fruit of the Spirit is love, joy, peace, forbearance, kindness, goodness, faithfulness, gentleness and self-control.* ~ Galatians 5:22–23

21. *You can give without loving, but you can never love without giving.* ~ Robert Louis Stevenson

22. *Never believe that a few caring people can't change the world. For, indeed, that's all who ever have.* ~ Margaret Mead

23. *Let us always meet each other with smile, for the smile is the beginning of love.* ~ Mother Teresa

24. *Never look down on anybody unless you're helping him up.* ~ Jesse Jackson

25. *Do to others as you would have them do to you.* ~ Luke 6:31

26. *Kindness is a language which the deaf can hear and the blind can see.* ~ Mark Twain

27. *Too often we underestimate the power of a touch, a smile, a kind word, a listening ear, an honest compliment, or the smallest act of caring, all of which have the potential to turn a life around.* ~ Leo Buscaglia

28. *As I get older, I realize that the thing I value the most is good-heartedness.* ~ Alice Walker

29. *I always prefer to believe the best of everybody; it saves so much trouble.* ~ Rudyard Kipling

30. *Three things in human life are important. The first is to be kind. The second is to be kind. And the third is to be kind.* ~ Henry James

31. *Be kind, for everyone you meet is fighting a harder battle.* ~ Plato

April: Courage and Strength

1. *If you're afraid to do it, do it afraid.* ~ The Hurt Healer

2. *Courage is resistance to fear, mastery of fear, not absence of fear.* ~ Mark Twain

3. *Fear defeats more people than any other one thing in the world.* ~ Ralph Waldo Emerson

4. *If you're captive of your past, living with an anxiety-filled present or dreading the future, then learning how to live fearlessly will set you free.* ~ The Hurt Healer

5. *For when I am weak, then I am strong.* ~ 2 Corinthians 12:10

6. *We may get knocked down on the outside, but the key to living in victory is to learn how to get up on the inside.* ~ Joel Osteen

7. *I'd rather stumble and fall than not try at all.* ~ The Hurt Healer

8. *The purpose exceeds the pain.* ~ Beth Moore

9. *So we can confidently say, "The Lord is my helper; I will not fear; what can man do to me?"*
   ~ Hebrews 13:6

10. *Sometimes our first and greatest dare is asking for support.* ~ Brené Brown

11. *Whatever you think you can do or believe you can do, begin it. Action has magic, grace, and power in it.*
    ~ Goethe

12. *You may believe that you haven't the strength or courage to overcome a situation that has overwhelmed you for so long. You do.* ~ The Hurt Healer

13. *For God has not given us a spirit of fear, but of power and of love and of a sound mind.* ~ 2 Timothy 1:7

14. *Be gentle, truthful, and fearless.* ~ Mahatma Gandhi

15. *Courage is not having the strength to go on; it is going on when you don't have the strength.*
    ~ Theodore Roosevelt

16. *We have to be braver than we think we can be, because God is constantly calling us to be more than we are.*
    ~ Madeleine L'Engle

17. *Tenderness and kindness are not signs of weakness and despair, but manifestations of strength and resolution.*
    ~ Khalil Gibran

18. *Set yourself free from "Why me?" It's time to say "Try me."* ~ The Hurt Healer

19. *So be strong and courageous, all you who put your hope in the LORD!* ~ Psalm 31:24

20. *Listen to what you know instead of what you fear.*
    ~ Richard Bach

21. *Embrace the fear of change and use it to fuel the excitement and anticipation of the good things to come.* ~ The Hurt Healer

22. *Keep your fears to yourself, but share your courage with others.* ~ Robert Louis Stevenson

23. *It takes courage to grow up and become who you really are.* ~ E. E. Cummings

24. *Act as if what you do makes a difference. It does.* ~ William James

25. *I have told you these things, so that in me you may have peace. In this world you will have trouble. But take heart! I have overcome the world.* ~ John 16:33

26. *Success is not final, failure is not fatal: it is the courage to continue that counts.* ~ Winston Churchill

27. *I learned that courage was not the absence of fear, but the triumph over it. The brave man is not he who does not feel afraid, but he who conquers that fear.* ~ Nelson Mandela

28. *Nothing in life is to be feared. It is only to be understood.* ~ Marie Curie

29. *I believe that the most important single thing, beyond discipline and creativity, is daring to dare.* ~ Maya Angelou

30. *You have power over your mind – not outside events. Realize this, and you will find strength.* ~ Marcus Aurelius

May: Healing

1. *When I reclaimed my heart, I reclaimed my life.*
   ~ The Hurt Healer

2. *Meditation can help us embrace our worries, our fear, our anger; and that is very healing. We let our own natural capacity of healing do the work.*
   ~ Thich Nhat Hanh

3. *We have been called to heal wounds, to unite what has fallen apart, and to bring home those who have lost their way.* ~ Francis of Assisi

4. *It's love that hurts and love that heals.*
   ~ The Hurt Healer

5. *Find a place inside where there's joy and the joy will burn out the pain.* ~ Joseph Campbell

6. *When you reach out to those you need to forgive, it is you that will be touched and healed.* ~ Bryant McGill

7. *Healing is a matter of time, but it is sometimes also a matter of opportunity.* ~ Hippocrates

8. *He heals the broken-hearted and binds up their wounds.*
   ~ Psalm 147:3

9. *It's not the wound that teaches, but the healing.*
   ~ Marty Rubin

10. *It is a curious sensation: the sort of pain that goes mercifully beyond our powers of feeling. When your heart is broken, your boats are burned: nothing matters any more. It is the end of happiness and the beginning of peace.* ~ George Bernard Shaw

11. *There were times my heart broke into painful fragments; then my soul perseveringly gathered an*

ocean of strength on my voyage towards renewal. ~
Angelica Hopes

12. *The wound is the place where the Light enters you.* ~
Rumi

13. *Healing requires from us to stop struggling, but to
enjoy life more and endure it less.* ~ Darina Stoyanova

14. *Changing is not just changing the things outside of us.
First of all we need the right view that transcends all
notions, including of being and non-being, creator and
creature, mind and spirit. That kind of insight is crucial
for transformation and healing.* ~ Thich Nhat Hanh

15. *As long as I have a heart I can heal, as long as I can heal
I have a heart.* ~ The Hurt Healer

16. *He restores my soul.* ~ Psalms 23:3

17. *Our wounds are often the openings into the best and
most beautiful part of us.* ~ David Richo

18. *Our sorrows and wounds are healed only when we
touch them with compassion.* ~ Buddha

19. *What is to give light must endure burning.*
~ Viktor E. Frankl

20. *Although the world is full of suffering, it is also full of
the overcoming of it.* ~ Helen Keller

21. *Oh what a wonderful soul so bright inside you. Got
power to heal the sun's broken heart, power to restore
the moon's vision too.* ~ Aberjhani

22. *Heal me, LORD, and I will be healed.*
~ Jeremiah 17:14

23. *Reject your sense of injury and the injury itself
disappears.* ~ Marcus Aurelius

24. *Your pain is the breaking of the shell that encloses your understanding.* ~ Khalil Gibran

25. *An affirmation to say everyday: "The healing power of God is working in me right now. Every day I get better and better in every way."* ~ Joyce Meyer

26. *Eventually you will come to understand that love heals everything, and love is all there is.* ~ Gary Zukav

27. *Grief can be the garden of compassion. If you keep your heart open through everything, your pain can become your greatest ally in your life's search for love and wisdom.* ~ Rumi

28. *As soon as healing takes place, go out and heal somebody else.* ~ Maya Angelou

29. *Gracious words are a honeycomb, sweet to the soul and healing to the bones.* ~ Proverbs 16:23–25

30. *All healing is first a healing of the heart.* ~ Carl Townsend

31. *In the depth of winter, I finally learned that within me there lay an invincible summer.* ~ Albert Camus

June: Serenity

1. *He who lives in harmony with himself lives in harmony with the universe.* ~ Marcus Aurelius

2. *Women need real moments of solitude and self-reflection to balance out how much of ourselves we give away.* ~ Barbara De Angelis

3. *The Lord turn his face toward you and give you peace.* ~ Numbers 6:26

4. *It isn't enough to talk about peace. One must believe in it. And it isn't enough to believe in it. One must work at it.* ~ Eleanor Roosevelt

5. *Do not be anxious about anything, but in everything, by prayer and petition, with thanksgiving, present your requests to God. And the peace of God, which transcends all understanding, will guard your hearts and your minds in Christ Jesus.* ~ Philippians 4:6–7

6. *Only your surface is disturbed; in your deepness there is stillness and total tranquility.*

   ~ Bryant McGill

7. *God grant me the serenity to accept the things I cannot change; courage to change the things I can; and wisdom to know the difference.*
   ~ Reinhold Niebuhr

8. *First keep the peace within yourself, then you can also bring peace to others.* ~ Thomas à Kempis

9. *Let all that I am wait quietly before God, for my hope is in him.* ~ Psalm 62:5

10. *If half a century of living has taught me anything at all, it has taught me that nothing can bring you peace but yourself.* ~ Dale Carnegie

11. *Only the development of compassion and understanding for others can bring us the tranquility and happiness we all seek.*
    ~ Dalai Lama

12. *Peace is not merely a distant goal that we seek but a means by which we arrive at that goal.* ~ Martin Luther King

13. *And you would accept the seasons of your heart just as you have always accepted that seasons pass over your fields and you would watch with serenity through the winters of your grief.*
~ Khalil Gibran.

14. *Our life is frittered away by detail ... simplify, simplify.*
~ Henry David Thoreau

15. *May the Lord of peace himself give you peace at all times and in every way. The Lord be with all of you.* ~ 2 Thessalonians 3:16

16. *Cheerfulness keeps up a kind of daylight in the mind, filling it with a steady and perpetual serenity.* ~ Joseph Addison

17. *When everything has its proper place in our minds, we are able to stand in equilibrium with the rest of the world.* ~ Henri-Frédéric Amiel

18. *In your serenity there is a clarity, strength, and correctness that is beyond the petty scuffles of the moment – a greater truth. It is the truth of who you are; beautiful, calm, secure, open, willing, and safe.* ~ Bryant McGill

19. *Go to sleep in peace. God is awake.* ~ Victor Hugo

20. *Never respond to an angry person with a fiery comeback, even if he deserves it ... Don't allow his anger to become your anger.* ~ Bohdi Sanders

21. *Nothing is so aggravating as calmness.*
~ Mahatma Gandhi

22. *Those who are at war with others are not at peace with themselves.* ~ William Hazlitt

23. *Whether it is serenity or energy that you seek, may you find it in abundance within the sanctuary of your soul.* ~ The Hurt Healer

24. *Pray silently with simplicity every day to stay cool and calm in mind, composed and collected in heart, courageous and connected to own soul, to lay the way for a peaceful life.* ~ Anuj Somany

25. *It is always in the midst, in the epicenter, of your troubles that you find serenity.* ~ Antoine de Saint-Exupéry

26. *The quieter you become, the more you can hear.* ~ Ram Dass.

27. *Where there is peace and meditation, there is neither anxiety nor doubt.* ~ Francis of Assisi

28. *Peace of mind is attained not by ignoring problems, but by solving them.* ~ Raymond Hull.

29. *Nothing can bring you peace but yourself. Nothing can bring you peace but the triumph of principles.* ~ Ralph Waldo Emerson

30. *Peace I leave with you; my peace I give you.* ~ John 14:27

July: Forgiveness

1. *The weak can never forgive. Forgiveness is the attribute of the strong.* ~ Mahatma Gandhi

2. *If you can't forgive yourself, you can't forgive others.* ~ The Hurt Healer

3. *There is no love without forgiveness, and there is no forgiveness without love.* ~ Bryant McGill

4. *He who cannot forgive breaks the bridge over which he himself must pass.* ~ George Herbert

5. *There is a difference between being compassionate and being spineless; between being forgiving and being used.* ~ The Hurt Healer

6. *Forgiveness does not change the past, but it does enlarge the future.* ~ Paul Boese

7. *While you will never forget, you can learn how to keep yourself from dwelling on it every single day.* ~ Sandi Krakowski

8. *A heartfelt apology from a place of love can heal the deepest wounds.* ~ The Hurt Healer

9. *Forgive yourself your faults and mistakes and move on.* ~ Les Brown

10. *To truly forgive is to allow the other person to forget.* ~ Robert Brault

11. *We think that forgiveness is weakness, but it's absolutely not; it takes a very strong person to forgive.* ~ T. D. Jakes

12. *If you can, help others; if you cannot do that, at least do not harm them.* ~ Dalai Lama

13. *True forgiveness is when you can say, "Thank you for that experience."* ~ Oprah Winfrey

14. *The truth is, unless you let go, unless you forgive yourself, unless you forgive the situation, unless you realize that the situation is over, you cannot move forward.* ~ Steve Maraboli

15. *Forgiveness is the remission of sins. For it is by this that what has been lost, and was found, is saved from being lost again.* ~ Saint Augustine

16. *Forgiveness is not always easy. At times, it feels more painful than the wound we suffered, to forgive the one that inflicted it. And yet, there is no peace without forgiveness.* ~ Marianne Williamson

17. *To forgive is to set a prisoner free and discover that the prisoner was you.* ~ Lewis B. Smedes

18. *Always forgive your enemies – nothing annoys them so much.* ~ Oscar Wilde

19. *You can't forgive without loving. And I don't mean sentimentality. I don't mean mush. I mean having enough courage to stand up and say, "I forgive. I'm finished with it."* ~ Maya Angelou

20. *Life is an adventure in forgiveness.* ~ Norman Cousins

21. *Forgiveness is an act of the will, and the will can function regardless of the temperature of the heart.* ~ Corrie ten Boom

22. *Forgive yourself for your faults and your mistakes and move on.* ~ Les Brown

23. *The more you are able to forgive then the more you are able to love.* ~ Stephen Richards

24. *And when you stand praying, if you hold anything against anyone, forgive them, so that your Father in heaven may forgive you your sins.* ~ Mark 11:25

25. *Forgiveness is for yourself because it frees you. It lets you out of that prison you put yourself in.* ~ Louise L. Hay

26. *Forgiveness says you are given another chance to make a new beginning.* ~ Desmond Tutu

27. *Forgiving is rediscovering the shining path of peace that at first you thought others took away when they betrayed you.* ~ Dodinsky

28. *To be wronged is nothing, unless you continue to remember it.* ~ Confucius

29. *If we can find forgiveness in our hearts for those who have caused us hurt and injury, we will rise to a higher level of self-esteem and well-being.* ~ James E. Faust

30. *Forgiveness is not a form of acceptance or surrender. It is a battle cry. Another person's actions have already stolen enough from me and I am refusing to let them take any more.* ~ The Hurt Healer

31. *Forgiveness is not an occasional act, it is a constant attitude.* ~ Martin Luther King

August: Happiness and Joy

1. *I have decided to be happy because it is good for my health* ~ Voltaire

2. *Happiness is a perfume you can't pour on others without getting a few drops on yourself.* ~ Ralph Waldo Emerson

3. *Joyful moments gracefully string together by trust, gratitude, inspiration, and faith.* ~ Brené Brown

4. *Dare to expose your vulnerability and you will reveal the intense beauty of your authenticity.* ~ The Hurt Healer

5. *He is richest who is content with the least, for content is the wealth of nature.* ~ Socrates

6. *The thief comes only in order to steal and kill and destroy. I came that they may have and enjoy life, and have it in abundance (to the full, till it overflows).* ~ John 10:10

7. *Happiness depends upon ourselves.* ~ Aristotle

8. *There is no real and true Joy if that Joy is not imbued with love. Love cannot exist without Joy.* ~ Saraydarian

9. *Sometimes your joy is the source of your smile, but sometimes your smile can be the source of your joy.* ~ Thich Nhat Hanh

10. *You are the only person who can make yourself happy, so think again if you are relying on someone else to make you feel good.* ~ The Hurt Healer

11. *Keep your face to the sunshine and you cannot see a shadow.* ~ Helen Keller

12. *Whoever is happy will make others happy too.* ~ Anne Frank

13. *Your word is a lamp for my feet, a light on my path.* ~ Psalm 119:105

14. *Happiness is infectious, so keep near to bright, cheerful souls and catch hold of the light.* ~ The Hurt Healer

15. *Always have a smile on your face, kind words on your lips and a compassionate heart.* ~ Amma

16. *It is in your spirit that you find love for others and in your soul that find love for yourself.* ~ The Hurt Healer

17. *Most of the shadows of this life are caused by standing in one's own sunshine.* ~ Ralph Waldo Emerson

18. *A new day: Be open enough to see opportunities. Be wise enough to be grateful. Be courageous enough to be happy.* ~ Steve Maraboli

19. *From the darkness of today, it is possible for a brighter tomorrow to emerge.* ~ The Hurt Healer

20. *If you are not living in Joy, you are out of integrity with your Soul.* ~ Michael Bernard Beckwith

21. *True happiness is living life authentically.* ~ The Hurt Healer

22. *The happiness of your life depends upon the quality of your thoughts.* ~ Marcus Aurelius

23. *If you want others to be happy, practice compassion. If you want to be happy, practice compassion.* ~ Dalai Lama

24. *Knock on the inner door. No other will take you to Joy.* ~ Rumi

25. *He is a wise man who does not grieve for the things which he has not, but rejoices for those which he has.* ~ Epictetus

26. *For every minute you are angry you lose sixty seconds of happiness.* ~ Ralph Waldo Emerson

27. *Happiness lies in the joy of achievement and the thrill of creative effort.* ~ Franklin D. Roosevelt

28. *A joyful heart is the inevitable result of a heart burning with love.* ~ Mother Teresa

29. *Success is getting what you want. Happiness is wanting what you get.* ~ Dale Carnegie

30. *Happiness is when what you think, what you say, and what you do are in harmony.* ~ Mahatma Gandhi

31. *Joy is prayer; joy is strength; joy is love; joy is a net of love by which you can catch souls.* ~ Mother Teresa

September: Inner Peace

1. *Breathe and let be.* ~ Jon Kabat-Zinn

2. *You give but little when you give of your possessions. It is when you give of yourself that you truly give.* ~ Khalil Gibran

3. *If you are depressed you are living in the past. If you are anxious you are living in the future. If you are at peace you are living in the present.* ~ Lao Tzu

4. *Start believing in yourself and reach for that inner strength that is waiting to be released.* ~ The Hurt Healer

5. *Do not judge yourself harshly. Without mercy for ourselves we cannot love the world.* ~ Buddha

6. *Nobody can hurt me without my permission.* ~ Mahatma Gandhi

7. *Once we realize that imperfect understanding is the human condition there is no shame in being wrong, only in failing to correct our mistakes.* ~ George Soros

8. *To live is to suffer, to survive is to find some meaning in the suffering.* ~ Friedrich Nietzsche

9. *When we feel whole in ourselves there is no need or desire to present ourselves as anything other than simply being.* ~ Catherine Ingram

10. *If you don't like something, change it. If you can't change it, change your attitude.* ~ Maya Angelou

11. *As soon as you refuse to give into the darkness, the light will reveal itself.* ~ The Hurt Healer

12. *Come to me, all you who are weary and burdened, and I will give you rest.* ~ Matthew 11:28

13. *May the passion to be all that God wants you to be sweep across your soul like a gentle breeze.* ~ T. D. Jakes

14. *When you are content to be simply yourself and don't compare or compete, everyone will respect you.* ~ Lao Tzu

15. *Peace is present right here and now, in ourselves and in everything we do and see. Every breath we take, every step we take, can be filled with peace, joy, and serenity.* ~ Thich Nhat Hanh

16. *Put down those bags crammed with destructive negativity. Leave and don't look back. You don't need them anymore.* ~ The Hurt Healer

17. *Looking deeply at life as it is in this very moment, the meditator dwells in stability and freedom.* ~ Buddha

18. *Never be in a hurry; do everything quietly and in a calm spirit. Do not lose your inner peace for anything whatsoever, even if your whole world seems upset.* ~ Francis de Sales

19. *When you lose touch with inner stillness, you lose touch with yourself. When you lose touch with yourself, you lose yourself in the world.* ~ Eckhart Tolle

20. *Freedom is what you do with what's been done to you.* ~ Jean-Paul Sartre

21. *Peace comes from within. Do not seek it without.* ~ Buddha

22. *Forget regret, or life is yours to miss.* ~ Jonathan Larson

23. *New beginnings are often disguised as painful endings.* ~ Lao Tzu

24. *Reach into your unconscious and become consciously inspired.* ~ The Hurt Healer

25. *We can never obtain peace in the outer world until we make peace with ourselves.* ~ Dalai Lama

26. *Pleasure is always derived from something outside you, whereas joy arises from within.* ~ Eckhart Tolle

27. *Negative emotions like hatred destroy our peace of mind.* ~ Matthieu Ricard

28. *People are like stained-glass windows. They sparkle and shine when the sun is out, but when the darkness sets in their true beauty is revealed only if there is light from within.* ~ Elisabeth Kübler-Ross

29. *Your sacred space is where you can find yourself over and over again.* ~ Joseph Campbell

30. *Saturate your thoughts with peaceful experiences, peaceful words and ideas, and ultimately you will have a storehouse of peace-producing experiences to which you may turn for refreshment and renewal of your spirit.* ~ Norman Vincent Peale

October: Hopes and Dreams

1. *Hope is the companion of power, and mother of success; for who so hopes strongly has within him the gift of miracles.* ~ Samuel Smiles

2. *Rejoice in hope, be patient in tribulation, be constant in prayer.* ~ Romans 12:12

3. *The gift of grace allows you to accept yesterday, live for today, and dream for tomorrow.* ~ The Hurt Healer

4. *The greater danger for most of us lies not in setting our aim too high and falling short; but in setting our aim too low, and achieving our mark.*
~ Michelangelo

5. *There is only one thing that makes a dream impossible to achieve: the fear of failure.* ~ Paulo Coelho

6. *Hope is the dream of the waking man.* ~ Aristotle

7. *This year I'm choosing to live beyond my wildest dreams. I wonder where they'll take me?* ~ Oprah Winfrey

8. *Dream Big. Start small. Act now.* ~ Robin Sharma.

9. *What you get by achieving your goals is not as important as what you become by achieving your goals.* ~ Henry David Thoreau

10. *You're something between a dream and a miracle.* ~ Elizabeth Barrett Browning

11. *What seems to us as bitter trials are often blessings in disguise.* ~ Oscar Wilde

12. *Yesterday is but today's memory, and tomorrow is today's dream.* ~ Khalil Gibran

13. *Resolve to be stronger than the pain of yesterday, find peace for today and pursue your dreams for tomorrow.* ~ The Hurt Healer

14. *"If you have built castles in the air, your work need not be lost; that is where they should be. Now put the foundations under them.* ~ Henry David Thoreau

15. *Take delight in the Lord, and he will give you the desires of your heart.* ~ Psalm 37:4

16. *You are never too old to set another goal or to dream a new dream.* ~ C. S. Lewis

17. *Without leaps of imagination, or dreaming, we lose the excitement of possibilities. Dreaming, after all, is a form of planning.* ~ Gloria Steinem

18. *Not every vision has to be a huge life-changing event. Little steps are just as significant. Big or small, it's never too late to dream.* ~ The Hurt Healer

19. *Only in the darkness can you see the stars.* ~ Martin Luther King

20. *God puts rainbows in the clouds so that each of us – in the dreariest and most dreaded moments – can see a possibility of hope.* ~ Maya Angelou

21. *Discover your calling and you will start to experience the ecstasy of an inspired life.* ~ Robin Sharma

22. *There is nothing like a dream to create the future.* ~ Victor Hugo

23. *The difference between average people and achieving people is their perception of and response to failure.* ~ John C. Maxwell

24. *The future belongs to those who believe in the beauty of their dreams.* ~ Eleanor Roosevelt

25. *Optimism is the faith that leads to achievement; nothing can be done without hope.* ~ Helen Keller

26. *Let your hopes, not your hurts, shape your future.* ~ Robert H. Schuller

27. *Clouds come floating into my life, no longer to carry rain or usher storm, but to add color to my sunset sky.* ~ Rabindranath Tagore

28. *You cannot expect victory and plan for defeat.* ~ Joel Osteen

29. *Hope is being able to see that there is light despite all of the darkness.* ~ Desmond Tutu

30. *Hope itself is like a star – not to be seen in the sunshine of prosperity, and only to be discovered in the night of adversity.* ~ Charles H. Spurgeon

31. *"For I know the plans I have for you," declares the Lord, "plans to prosper you and not to harm you, plans to give you hope and a future."*
~ Jeremiah 29:11

November: Gratitude

1. *Wake at dawn with winged heart and give thanks for another day of loving.* ~ Khalil Gibran

2. *It is through gratitude for the present moment that the spiritual dimension of life opens up.* ~ Eckhart Tolle

3. *O give thanks to the LORD, for He is good; For His loving kindness is everlasting.*
    ~ 1 Chronicles 16:34

4. *If we magnified blessings as much as we magnify disappointments, we would all be much happier.* ~ John Wooden

5. *Gratitude is the sign of noble souls.* ~ Aesop

6. *I don't have to chase extraordinary moments to find happiness – it's right in front of me if I'm paying attention and practicing gratitude.* ~ Brené Brown

7. *Gratitude is not only the greatest of virtues, but the parent of all the others.* ~ Cicero

8. *The unthankful heart discovers no mercies; but the thankful heart will find, in every hour, some heavenly blessings.* ~ Henry Ward Beecher

9. *Gratitude is a great pain-killer.* ~ The Hurt Healer

10. *Gratitude is something of which none of us can give too much. For on the smiles, the thanks we give, our little gestures of appreciation, our neighbors build their philosophy of life.*
    ~ A. J. Cronin

11. *Appreciation is the purest vibration that exists on the planet today.* ~ Abraham-Hicks

12. *Feeling gratitude and not expressing it is like wrapping a present and not giving it.* ~ William Arthur Ward

13. *Gratitude helps you to grow and expand; gratitude brings joy and laughter into your life and into the lives of all those around you.* ~ Eileen Caddy

14. *Let us serve the world soulfully. The pay we will receive for our service will be in the currency of gratitude. God's gratitude.* ~ Sri Chinmoy

15. *As we express our gratitude, we must never forget that the highest appreciation is not to utter words, but to live by them.* ~ John F. Kennedy

16. *Gratitude is medicine for a heart devastated by tragedy. If you can only be thankful for the blue sky, then do so.* ~ Richelle E. Goodrich

17. *Gratitude is the memory of the heart.* ~ Jean Baptiste Massieu

18. *Do not indulge in dreams of having what you have not, but reckon up the chief of the blessings you do possess, and then thankfully remember how you would crave for them if they were not yours.* ~ Marcus Aurelius

19. *Gratitude dissolves so much negativity. Make a decision today that no matter what comes your way, you'll find a grateful heart.* ~ Sandi Krakowski

20. *The grateful heart sits at a continuous feast.* ~ Proverbs 15:15

21. *Rest and be thankful.* ~ William Wordsworth

22. *I would maintain that thanks are the highest form of thought; and that gratitude is happiness doubled by wonder.* ~ G. K. Chesterton

23. *The smallest act of kindness is worth more than the grandest intention.* ~ Oscar Wilde

24. *Let us rise up and be thankful; for if we didn't learn a lot today, at least we learned a little, and if we didn't learn a little, at least we didn't get sick, and if we got sick, at least we didn't die; so, let us all be thankful.* ~ Buddha

25. *Happiness doesn't come as a result of getting something we don't have, but of recognizing and appreciating what we do have.* ~ Friedrich Koenig

26. *I thank my God always when I remember you in my prayers.* ~ Philemon 1:4

27. *You pray in your distress and in your need; would that you might pray also in the fullness of your joy and in your days of abundance.* ~ Khalil Gibran

28. *If you concentrate on finding whatever is good in every situation, you will discover that your life will suddenly be filled with gratitude, a feeling that nurtures the soul.* ~ Rabbi Harold Kushner

29. *We can only be said to be alive in those moments when our hearts are conscious of our treasures.* ~ Thornton Wilder

30. *This is the day which the LORD has made; we will rejoice and be glad in it.* ~ Psalms 118:24

December: Faith and Spirituality

1. *Pour out your heart before Him. God is a refuge for us.* ~ Psalm 62:8

2. *Faith is like a bird that feels dawn breaking and sings while it is dark.* ~ Rabindranath Tagore

3. *Hope keeps you alive. Faith gives your life meaning, blessings, and a good end.* ~ Rex Rouis

4. *Today I know the truth of who I am because I live in the Truth.* ~ The Hurt Healer

5. *Faith consists in believing when it is beyond the power of reason to believe.* ~ Voltaire

6. *Spirit is an invisible force made visible in all life.* ~ Maya Angelou

7. *A little faith will bring your soul to heaven, but a lot of faith will bring heaven to your soul.* ~ Dwight L. Moody

8. *To one who has faith, no explanation is necessary. To one without faith, no explanation is possible.* ~ Thomas Aquinas

9. *The beginning of anxiety is the end of faith, and the beginning of true faith is the end of anxiety.* ~ George Müller

10. *Faith is believing the unimaginable; reaching the unattainable and dreaming the impossible.* ~ The Hurt Healer

11. *Now faith is being sure of what we hope for and certain of what we do not see.* ~ Hebrews 11:1

12. *Let my soul smile through my heart and my heart smile through my eyes, that I may scatter rich smiles in sad hearts.* ~ Paramahansa Yogananda

13. *The best way to know God is to love many things.* ~ Vincent van Gogh

14. *Faith is the strength by which a shattered world shall emerge into light.* ~ Helen Keller

15. *No eye has seen, no ear has heard, and no mind has imagined the things that God has prepared for those who love him.* ~ 1 Corinthians 2:9

16. *Faith taught me that just as love hurts, so does it heal.* ~ The Hurt Healer

17. *If there is light in the soul, there will be beauty in the person.* ~ Chinese Proverb

18. *Faith is a knowledge within the heart, beyond the reach of proof.* ~ Khalil Gibran

19. *Peace I leave with you; my peace I give you. I do not give to you as the world gives. Do not let your hearts be troubled and do not be afraid.* ~ John 14:27

20. *I'm not where I need to be, but thank God I'm not where I used to be. I'm OK, and I'm on my way!* ~ Joyce Meyer

21. *I found my serenity by focusing on the tiniest speck of light that gave me a whisper of hope. That little speck of light was faith.* ~ The Hurt Healer

22. *My flesh and my heart may fail, but God is the strength of my heart and my portion forever.* ~ Psalm 73:26

23. *Have faith in God; God has faith in you.* ~ Edwin Louis Cole

24. *I have just three things to teach: simplicity, patience, compassion. These three are your greatest treasures.* ~ Lao Tzu

25. *Therefore I tell you, whatever you ask for in prayer, believe that you have received it, and it will be yours.* ~ Mark 11:24

26. *Never doubt in the dark what God has shown you in the light.* ~ Edith Edman

27. *The spiritual life does not remove us from the world but leads us deeper into it* ~ Henri J. M. Nouwen

28. *May God give you … For every storm a rainbow, for every tear a smile, for every care a promise and a blessing in each trial. For every problem life sends, a faithful friend to share, for every sigh a sweet song and an answer for each prayer.* ~ Irish blessing

29. *Whoever has God lacks nothing; God alone suffices.* ~ Teresa of Ávila

30. *Faith is taking the first step even when you don't see the whole staircase.* ~ Martin Luther King

31. *May the God of hope fill you with all joy and peace as you trust in him, so that you may overflow with hope by the power of the Holy Spirit.* ~ Romans 15:13

About the Author: Carolyn Hughes's Story

When I look back at how my life used to be, it's almost impossible to believe the transformation. Overcoming depression has been a long process, but it's been worth it, because today I live my life as the person I know I was meant to be. It's a vast difference from the desperate alcoholic that I once was.

How it started

I was born in Balham, London, where my family lived the first few years of my life. One of my earliest recollections was going to the park with my mother. She'd sit on a bench and I'd run to a huge tree that was in the middle of the grass, wave at her, then run back, and she'd give me a big hug. Then I'd do it all over again. I guess I thought she'd always be there for me to run back to. But that park was actually the very place she abandoned me.

I was three when one day my mum simply left me on a park bench. I'll never know how long I sat there before a family friend came to collect me. I wasn't scared; I knew the woman who came for me and I was happy to go with her—I had no reason to doubt my mum. It simply never occurred to me that she had left me.

I can't remember when it hit me that she wasn't coming back. It was a slow realization because, as odd as it still seems to me now, no one mentioned her. I was brought home to my father and suddenly it was as if my mother didn't exist. For years there was just complete silence

81

about her disappearance and if I dared ask, the subject was changed. My mother was from France, so we didn't really have much contact with her family, but if we did hear from them they pretended she didn't exist too.

Like all children who are victims of an adult decision, I blamed myself for what had happened. By that time I was certain of two things: my mum had left me because I was bad, and because she didn't love me. Yet I grew up holding tight to the dream that she would come back and prove me wrong.

I never saw her again. To this day I have no idea why she left.

Sadly, my mother's abandonment is only a small part of the story about how I ended up a depressed, anxious adult with no confidence. The worst thing about her leaving was that I was left with my father.

Although I was given no reasons why my mother left, my father used her disappearance as an excuse for anything and everything. I was a very timid and nervous child and whenever teachers expressed their concern, my dad automatically blamed my mother. "She's like that because her mother left her," he was fond of saying. And when he was being critical of me it was always: "It's no wonder your mum left you." Or: "No one will ever love you. Your mother never did." And then there was: "You're so like your mother."

No wonder I blamed myself!

I didn't tell anyone about the things my father said. He was a very charming man, admired by others for raising me alone (not common in the 1970s), so who would have believed me anyway? Who would have known that he was a manipulative man who thrived on demeaning and degrading others?

He had a particular hatred of women. I remember being told off by a primary school teacher because I was trying to find a word in the dictionary, a name that my father had called me. I had been looking at words beginning with "H" and asked my teacher how to spell "whore." She just thought I was being rude and naughty; I didn't dare tell her the truth.

As I got older, it was my looks that my father picked on. As a teenager he was obsessed with me having a waist that was twenty-two inches, but mine was twenty-three; it wasn't good enough. As for schoolwork, if I got ninety-eight percent, he would focus on the two percent that I didn't get. To say he was controlling is an understatement. It shocks me now when I recall the way my father monitored me, but at the time I didn't know any different.

Everything was part of a deal. If I wanted to eat a certain food then I had to do something for him. Even when I moved out he would turn up wherever I was living and refuse to leave. I remember the first job I got after I finished my degree. I was so excited. He asked me how much they would be paying me, and when I told him, he replied, "You're not worth that." He would ring up the manager wherever it was I was working (particularly when I was a social worker) and tell them what a dreadful person I was and try to get me sacked.

As for any attempts I made to find love, I never stood a chance. My father did his best to sabotage any relationship I was in by intimidating my partner and making his life a misery, threatening him and turning up uninvited to sit outside his house. It sounds like the kind of thing you'd see in a movie, but it was actually my life.

So I grew up fearing everything and everybody, and believing I was worthless and unlovable. The foundations for a twenty-five year struggle with depression were firmly in place.

Being diagnosed as depressed

At the age of fourteen, I went on my own to our family doctor and told him how miserable I felt. He knew something of my family circumstances, although not the whole story (I was too scared to tell him), and he treated my symptoms on the basis that I was a teenage girl growing up without a mother. I was given tranquilizers.

When I was eighteen I went back and told him that I felt like killing myself. He was very supportive and acted immediately. I was admitted to hospital for a few days and put on antidepressants. Looking back, and having heard other people's stories, I think I was very fortunate to have had sympathetic doctors all my life.

Like many who suffer depression, mine was an ongoing condition that worsened during stressful or challenging life events. During the really bad episodes I was offered short-term psychotherapy and my medication was increased. This relieved my anxieties and raised my sense of well-being for a while, but the emotional scars ran deep and were going to require much more intensive intervention.

The effects of depression on my adult life

On the outside I appeared to be functioning as a successful adult. I was awarded a first degree (BA Hons.) in Applied Social Science (Psychology and Social Policy) and gained a professional qualification—Certificate in Qualification of Social Work (CQSW). I then worked for fifteen years as a children and families social worker in England and Germany. I found it easy to help others yet couldn't help myself. But in reality I was a very unhappy, troubled, isolated woman. It was like I was looking out from the inside of a goldfish bowl. I could see and hear everyone, but I couldn't connect.

Abandonment by my mother combined with the criticism I put up with from my father left me severely lacking in confidence and a fear of rejection that progressed into a fear of attachment. In other words, I couldn't do intimacy. I just couldn't develop relationships on anything more than a superficial level.

Even with friends I always kept my distance. At school and college I had a few close friends, but I'd often take time out to be on my own because I couldn't bear to be around people, especially if they seemed happy and were getting on with their lives. It just made me so aware that I was neither happy nor getting on with mine.

But I really struggled with intimate relationships. By the time my friends were getting married and settling down, I was still avoiding any commitment at all. I did try. When I was twenty I was briefly engaged, but I called the whole thing off because, even though I loved him, I told myself there must be more to life and that the marriage would just fail. And that became my pattern—I'd get into a serious relationship, convince myself it would all go wrong, and end it. So I gave up on serious relationships altogether and turned to alcohol.

Alcoholism and depression

My dad once remarked that he'd rather I got pregnant than drunk. I was around fourteen at the time and looking for any opportunity to rebel against him. So when I got the opportunity to try wine at a friend's house I didn't need any persuading. I loved it from the first sip.

When I was legally old enough to buy drink for myself (18 in the UK), my dad knew I was hooked. He hated it. But I was an adult and he could do nothing about it. I loved that it upset him.

Unfortunately, in my attempt to get back at him, I ended up abusing drink and becoming dependent. He never knew that I was drinking excessively before he died; by that time I couldn't have given up, even if I'd wanted to.

I see now that alcohol was my way to numb my emotional pain and help me feel more confident. By the time I was in my twenties I regularly spent whole weekends on my own getting drunk, comfort eating, and detaching from reality. My friends noticed and weren't at all surprised when I did eventually have a complete breakdown.

Breakdown

Inevitably the calming, soothing effects of drinking alcohol wore off. Alcohol is, of course, a depressant, so rather than alleviating my symptoms it began to make them worse.

But by that time it was too late. I couldn't stop—I'd crossed the line into dependency.

Looking back, I can see there was never anything social about my drinking—I always drank to get drunk. I drank regularly for five years in increasing amounts, and eventually I was drinking every day and night, from the moment I woke up in the morning to when I went to sleep at night.

Alcohol took me from feeling depressed to being suicidal. I looked terrible—my eyes were always bloodshot, I reeked of booze, I put on a couple of stone, and everything ached. During the last couple of years of my alcoholism I took more and more time off work, avoided friends, and generally hid from the world.

This lifestyle was a recipe for disaster on its own. But there were two major events that led to my eventual breakdown. The first was my decision to search for my mother when I was twenty-two. I had prepared myself for the fact that she might have another family, so that I was ready to deal with. I tracked down her second husband (it turned out that she hadn't had any more children with him), only to find that she'd abandoned her second family too—without a trace!

But nothing could have prepared me for the discovery that my mother had told everyone that her daughter—me—had been killed in a car crash and that she'd erased me from existence.

Hearing that she'd washed her hands of me wasn't enough to stop me trying to find her. I asked Salvation Army for help in tracing her (at the time they were the biggest organization that traced family members), but the problem was that if they successfully traced someone and that person said they didn't want to be found, the Salvation Army weren't allowed to pass on any information. In my case, they were never able to tell me for definite if they had found my mother, but I'm fairly certain they did and that she didn't want to have contact with me.

The second event that knocked me down was when my father died unexpectedly; I was twenty-seven. I'd always believed that his death would mean instant emotional healing and freedom, but I found instead that my depression intensified to a much deeper and darker level.

Eventually, I ended up off work for several months, when I got into terrible debt, drank heavily, and was dumped by the man I was with. And all that loss led to an alcohol-induced suicide attempt, followed by voluntary admission to a psychiatric ward where I stayed for several weeks: I'd also lost my will to live.

Getting my life back

Maybe some of us have to hit rock bottom before we're ready to come back up. There I was with only choice: to surrender to my illnesses or die from them. With the guidance and commitment of expert medical staff, I was able to admit that I struggled with depression and alcoholism. The stigmas of those issues were no longer relevant in my battle to survive, so I gave myself permission to hand over everything that was harming me.

Being in the hospital was pretty scary at first. They took me off all medication. What I remember most was crying for hours on end. But the nurses were kind, understanding, patient, and encouraging. I was surprised at the number of professionals who were patients there with me—a musician, a professor, a midwife. I guess I had my own set of prejudices about depression.

After my hospital stay I was fortunate enough to be offered a six-month spot in residential rehab that ran a faith-based twelve step program for women. Through intense group work—hard work—I gradually confronted my past and learned not only to accept what had happened, but to replace my mistaken perceptions with the truth. It was just what I needed. Reclaiming my faith also allowed me to get to a place of acceptance and forgiveness.

The upside to depression

While depression had brought me to the point of giving up, it was also the catalyst for my healing. It gave me the opportunity to work through my shame and to grasp the truth—that it was my choice to either live a better life or live as a prisoner of my past; that I was a lovable, good human being; that I was powerful.

Living my life as the person I was meant to be

My recovery has continued in the years since I left hospital and rehab in 1998, and I'm still on my journey. Learning how to love myself and then love someone else has been a big part of my healing process, as was learning how to forgive.

Today I take care of myself physically and emotionally. I eat healthily, exercise regularly, and get enough sleep. No matter how busy I am I always find a few minutes of serenity each day. Sometimes that's in prayer, or music, or reading a book. I'm also mindful of those triggers that can jeopardize my mental health or my sobriety, triggers such as confrontation or fatigue.

Now I can honestly say I love myself and my life. It's a life I share with great friends, inspiring colleagues, a wonderful husband (we met six months after I left rehab), and two amazing daughters who constantly inspire me to keep well and enjoy myself. It's good to be me.

This article originally featured on:
http://www.harleytherapy.co.uk/counselling/successfull y-overcoming-depression-case-study.htm#ixzz3HkaVmIvT

The Hurt Healer

For twenty years I called alcohol "The Hurt Healer" — it helped me numb the pain of the past, gave me confidence to deal with the present, and took away my fears for the future. Since 1998, when I left rehab, I have found freedom in sobriety and overcome long-term depression.

Having reclaimed my life, The Hurt Healer now means faith, love, serenity, joy, positivity and creativity. It's also the name I've given my business. Through The Hurt Healer website and blog, my aim is to help others with their addiction and mental health issues. I run one-to-one mentoring sessions via Skype and FaceTime, offering professional advice and solutions. In addition, I create and facilitate specialized small group workshops in personal development and life issues for a wide range of community, faith and women's organizations.

Based in the UK, I'm also a freelance writer. My inspirational posts and articles are regularly published in the UK and the United States.

How can I help? I'd love to hear from you.

How to contact me

Email: info@thehurthealer.com
Website: http://thehurthealer.com/
Facebook: https://www.facebook.com/TheHurtHealer
Twitter: https://twitter.com/TheHurtHealer
Pinterest: http://www.pinterest.com/TheHurtHealer
LinkedIn: https://www.linkedin.com/in/thehurthealer

Made in the USA
San Bernardino, CA
30 May 2015